IT'S ABOUT TIME!

It's About Time!

Poems Selected by
Lee Bennett Hopkins
Illustrated by Matt Novak

SIMON & SCHUSTER BOOKS FOR YOUNG READERS
Published by Simon & Schuster
New York • London • Toronto • Sydney • Tokyo • Singapore

To Alan Benjamin
because—
it's about time!
    —L.B.H.

For Mary
    —M.N.

SIMON & SCHUSTER BOOKS FOR YOUNG READERS. Simon & Schuster Building, Rockefeller Center, 1230 Avenue of the Americas, New York, New York 10020. Copyright © 1993 by Lee Bennett Hopkins. Illustrations copyright © 1993 by Matt Novak. All rights reserved including the right of reproduction in whole or in part in any form. SIMON & SCHUSTER BOOKS FOR YOUNG READERS is a trademark of Simon & Schuster.

Designed by David Neuhaus.
The text of this book is set in 14 pt. Palatino. The illustrations were done in colored pencil.

Manufactured in the United States of America.   10 9 8 7 6 5 4 3 2 1

Library of Congress Cataloging-in-Publication Data. It's about time / [compiled] by Lee Bennett Hopkins ; illustrated by Matt Novak.   p. cm. Summary: Sixteen poems by a variety of American poets reflect thoughts about time. 1. Time—Juvenile poetry. 2. Children's poetry, American. [1. Time—Poetry. 2. American poetry—Collections.] I. Hopkins, Lee Bennett. II. Novak, Matt, ill. PS595.T62I87 1993 811.008 09282—dc20 92-12128 CIP
ISBN: 0-671-78512-5

Contents

7:00 A.M.

from
All Kinds of Time

I have a face
and hands
and I can tell time
pretty well.
But I'm not a clock.
Nobody has to wind *me* up.
I go to sleep at night
and just wake up wound.

Harry Behn

7:30 A.M.

Before Breakfast

Mother has to comb her hair,
Father has to shave,
but I keep getting hungry
with the time I save.

Aileen Fisher

8:00 A.M.

See, I Can Do It

See, I can do it all myself
With my own little brush!
The tooth paste foams inside my mouth.
The faucet waters rush.

    In and out and underneath
    And round and round and round:
    First I do my upstairs teeth
    And then I do my down—

        The part I like the best of it
        Is at the end, though, when I spit.

Dorothy Aldis

13

8:30 A.M.

Shadows

Chunks of night
Melt
In the morning sun.
One lonely one
Grows legs
And follows me
To school.

Patricia Hubbell

15

10:00 A.M.

Writing on the Chalkboard

Up and down, my chalk goes.

Squeak, squeak, squeak!

Hush, chalk.

Don't squawk.

Talk *softly* when you speak.

Isabel Joshlin Glaser

16

12:00 P.M.

18

from
Company

I'm fixing a lunch for a dinosaur.
Who knows when one might come by?
I'm pulling up all the weeds I can find.
I'm piling them high as the sky.
I'm fixing a lunch for a dinosaur.
I hope he will stop by soon.
Maybe he'll just walk down my street
and have some lunch at noon.

Bobbi Katz

1:00 P.M.

Marie Lucille

The clock is ticking
Me away!
The me that only
Yesterday
Ate peanuts, jam and
Licorice
Is gone already.
And this is
'Cause nothing's putting
Back, each day,
The me that clock is
Ticking away.

Gwendolyn Brooks

2:30 P.M.

New Puppy

I can't *wait*
for school to be over,
can't *wait*
to rush down the street,

For I
have a new brown puppy
with funny white socks
for feet.

He's the wiggliest
bundle of wiggles
you ever
could hope to see.

I can't *wait* ...
and I hope my puppy
is waiting as hard
for me.

Aileen Fisher

4:00 P.M.

At the Table

Milk and cookies after school
    make homework fun to do.

I dunk
    subtract
        and take a bite

and carry   over two.

Constance Andrea Keremes

MATH
WORKSHEET 9

1. 2 + 2 = 4
2. 12 - 4 = 8
3. 10 + 3 = 13
4. 15 - 12 = 3
5. 80 - 19 = (crossed out)
6. 80 - 19 =
7. 43 + 9 = 52
8. 56 - 13 = ___
9. 12 + 7 = ___
10. 11 - 11 = ___

5:00 P.M.

There Isn't Time!

There isn't time, there isn't time
To do the things I want to do,
With all the mountain-tops to climb,
And all the woods to wander through,
And all the seas to sail upon,
And everywhere there is to go,
And all the people, every one
Who lives upon the earth, to know.
There's only time, there's only time
To know a few, and do a few,
And then sit down and make a rhyme
About the rest I want to do.

Eleanor Farjeon

6:00 P.M.

Some Bird

The sparrow
flew down
to the sidewalk
to stop my game of handball.

I wonder
if he heard my mother calling
me to supper for the
third time?

Lee Bennett Hopkins

29

Spaghetti! Spaghetti!

Spaghetti! spaghetti!
you're wonderful stuff,
I love you, spaghetti,
I can't get enough.
You're covered with sauce
and you're sprinkled with cheese,
spaghetti! spaghetti!
oh, give me some please.

Spaghetti! spaghetti!
piled high in a mound,
you wiggle, you wriggle,
you squiggle around.
There's slurpy spaghetti
all over my plate,
spaghetti! spaghetti!
I think you are great.

Spaghetti! spaghetti!
I love you a lot,
you're slishy, you're sloshy,
delicious and hot.
I gobble you down
oh, I can't get enough,
spaghetti! spaghetti!
you're wonderful stuff.

Jack Prelutsky

8:00 P.M.

32

from
Near the Window Tree

Wordless words.
A tuneless tune.
Blow out the sun.
Draw down the shade.
Turn off the dog.
Snap on the stars.
Unwrap the moon.
Wish leafy, sleeping trees good night
And listen
To the day shut tight.

Karla Kuskin

33

9:00 P.M.

Bedtime

Can I have a glass of water?
Can I sip some apple juice?
Can I say good night to Daddy?
Will you read me Dr. Seuss?

Will I see you in the morning?
Won't you please keep on the light?

Oh—
If only I could find a way
To chase
      away
         the
            night.

Lee Bennett Hopkins

9:30 P.M.

Bedtime Thoughts

The clock ticks the night away
Think of
      soft blue summer skies
Think of
      the garden, golden and sweet
Think of
      the bright world you'll wake to
      after tonight's cool sleep.

Charlotte Zolotow

12:00 A.M.

Time Passes

Sixty seconds
Pass in a minute.
Sixty minutes
Pass in an hour.
Twenty-four hours
Pass in a day—
And that's how TIME
Keeps passing away!

Ilo Orleans

ACKNOWLEDGMENTS

Thanks are due to the following for works reprinted herein:

Curtis Brown, Ltd. for "Bedtime" by Lee Bennett Hopkins. Revised version Copyright © 1993 by Lee Bennett Hopkins. Originally titled "Charlie's Bedtime" Copyright © 1972 by Lee Bennett Hopkins; "Some Bird" by Lee Bennett Hopkins. Copyright © 1972 by Lee Bennett Hopkins. Both reprinted by permission of Curtis Brown, Ltd.

Isabel Joshlin Glaser for "Writing on the Chalkboard." Used by permission of the author, who controls all rights.

HarperCollins Publishers for "Marie Lucille" from *Bronzeville Boys and Girls* by Gwendolyn Brooks. Copyright © 1956 by Gwendolyn Brooks Blakely; "There Isn't Time" from *Eleanor Farjeon's Poems for Children* by Eleanor Farjeon. Originally appeared in *Over the Garden Wall* by Eleanor Farjeon. Copyright 1933, renewed 1961 by Eleanor Farjeon; "Before Breakfast" from *In One Door and Out the Other* by Aileen Fisher. Copyright © 1969 by Aileen Fisher; "New Puppy" from *Feathered Ones and Furry* by Aileen Fisher. Text copyright © 1971 by Aileen Fisher; excerpt from *Near the Window Tree* by Karla Kuskin. Copyright © 1975 by Karla Kuskin. All reprinted by permission of HarperCollins Publishers.

Bobbi Katz for an excerpt from "Company" from *Upside Down and Inside Out: Poems for All Your Pockets*. Copyright © 1974 by Bobbi Katz. Used by permission of the author, who controls all rights.

Constance Andrea Keremes for "At the Table." Used by permission of the author, who controls all rights.

Macmillan Publishing Company for "Shadows" from *Catch Me A Wind* by Patricia Hubbell. Copyright © 1968 by Patricia Hubbell. Reprinted by permission of Atheneum Publishers, an imprint of Macmillan Publishing Company.

William Morrow and Company, Inc. for "Spaghetti! Spaghetti!" from *Rainy, Rainy Saturday* by Jack Prelutsky. Copyright © 1980 by Jack Prelutsky. By permission of Greenwillow Books, a division of William Morrow and Company, Inc.

The Putnam Publishing Group for "See, I Can Do It" from *All Together* by Dorothy Aldis. Copyright 1925-1928, 1934, 1939, 1952, © renewed 1953-1956, 1962 by Dorothy Aldis, © 1967 by Roy Porter. By permission of G. P. Putnam's Sons.

Marian Reiner for an excerpt from *All Kinds of Time* by Harry Behn. Copyright 1950 by Harry Behn. Copyright renewed 1978 by Alice Behn Goebel. Reprinted by permission of Marian Reiner.

Karen S. Solomon for "Time Passes" by Ilo Orleans.

Charlotte Zolotow for "Bedtime Thoughts." Used by permission of the author, who controls all rights.